# The Night Before Christmas

Candy Cane Press

An Imprint of
Ideals Publications Incorporated
Nashville, Tennessee

# The NIGHT Before CHRISTMAS

*The Classic Poem by*

## Clement Clarke Moore

*Illustrated by*

## Donald Mills

## Meet the Author

Clement Clarke Moore inadvertently defined an American image of Santa Claus when he wrote a short poem entitled "A Visit from St. Nicholas." Moore wrote the poem as a holiday gift to his children while riding in his sleigh to his estate outside of New York City.

Fluent in French, Italian, Greek, Latin, and Hebrew, Moore was a professor of Oriental and Greek literature at Columbia University; he was known for his serious writings on religion, literature, and education and was a wealthy and generous philanthropist. He was, however, also the father of nine children; and on that snowy evening in late December of 1822, he was thinking not of the classics of ancient Greece, but of a way to delight his children as they gathered around him on Christmas Eve.

The legend of St. Nicholas had been part of Christmas lore throughout the world for centuries. The Dutch who settled in New York brought St. Nicholas to America, but he did not become truly American until Moore fashioned for him a new identity. The physical traits Moore attributed to St. Nicholas were, ironically, modeled after an old Dutch handyman who worked on the family estate.

Moore never sought publication for his poem, never wished to have it read outside his home, and, for almost a quarter of a century, refused to publicly acknowledge authorship. A meddling friend ignored Moore's wishes to keep his poem in the family and sent it to a newspaper where it was anonymously published just before Christmas 1823. Within a few years, the poem became well known in almost every American home. From that time on, "The Night Before Christmas" found a place in the heart of every American child who cherished the hopes and dreams of Christmas.

Dr. Moore died in 1863 at the age of eighty-three and was buried in Trinity Cemetery in New York. The list of his published works is long, and all are scholarly treatises—except for one short poem. Moore, inspired by love for his children, gave a "right jolly old elf" to America, and, thus, to the world. Today, we can imagine no other vision of our beloved Santa Claus than that portrait so skillfully drawn by Clement Clarke Moore. And as for Santa's flying reindeer—why, of course they fly! How else would they get up to the rooftops?

## Meet the Illustrator

In 1961, Ideals asked artist Donald Mills to capture the whimsy and magic of Clement Clarke Moore's "The Night Before Christmas." The result was a series of watercolor images that brought the classic tale to life for a new generation of children to discover.

Born November 16, 1896, in Carrollton, Illinois, Donald Jackson Mills exhibited remarkable artistic talent as a young boy. With no prior art education, Mills matriculated at the prestigious Art Institute of Chicago at the age of seventeen. Through these years of extensive study and instruction, Mills developed a unique individual style, which was at once detailed yet subtle. Working in watercolors and pencils, he made use of value and light rather than line or brushstroke to define objects.

Mills's successful career as an illustrator spanned more than half a century, and he continued working until his death at his home in Evanston, Illinois, at the age of seventy-eight.

Perhaps Donald Mills's greatest contribution as an artist lay in his ability to tell a story in a single illustration, and nowhere is his talent more evident than in this delightful edition of "The Night Before Christmas."

'Twas the night
before Christmas,
when all through the house
Not a creature was stirring,
not even a mouse.

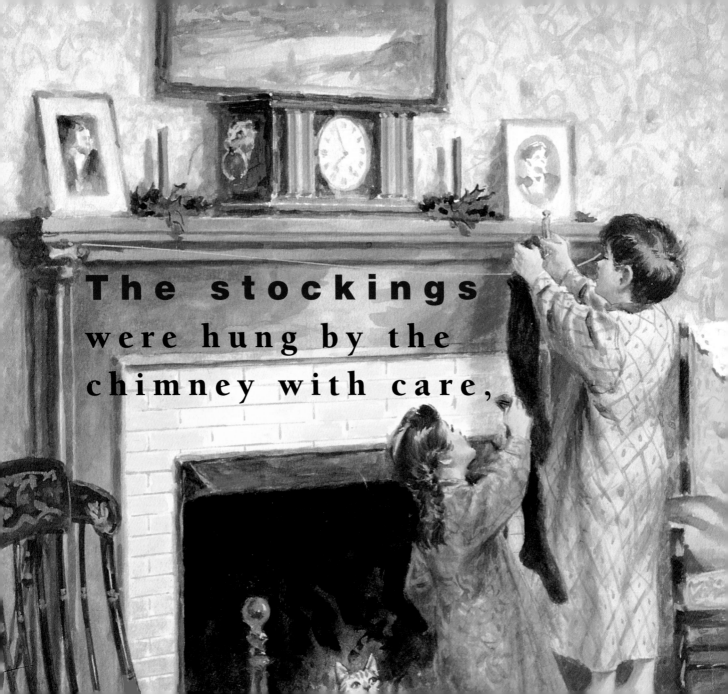

The stockings
were hung by the
chimney with care,

The children were nestled
all snug in their beds,
While visions of sugarplums
danced in their heads.

And Mama
in her
kerchief,
and I in
my cap,
Had just
settled
our brains
for a long winter's nap.

When out on the lawn
there arose
such a clatter,
I sprang from my bed
to see what
was the matter.

Away to the window
I flew like a flash,
Tore open the shutters
and threw up the sash.

The moon
on the
breast of the
new-fallen
**snow**
Gave a
luster
of midday
to objects
below.

When, what to my
wondering eyes
should appear,
But a miniature
sleigh
and eight tiny
reindeer,

With a little
old driver
so lively
and
quick,
I knew in
a moment
it must be
Saint Nick.

More rapid than eagles
his coursers they came,
And he whistled and shouted
and called them by name:

"Now, **Dasher!** Now, **Dancer!**
Now, Prancer and **Vixen!**
On, **Comet!** On, Cupid!
On, **Donder** and **Blitzen!**
To the top of the porch,
to the top of the wall!
Now, dash away! Dash away!
Dash away all!"

As dry leaves that before
the wild hurricane fly
When they meet
with an obstacle,
mount to the sky,

So up to **the housetop**
the coursers they flew
With **the sleigh full of toys,**
and *Saint Nicholas* too.
**And then in a twinkling**
I heard on the roof
The prancing and pawing
**of each little hoof.**

As I drew in
my head and
was turning
around,
Down the
chimney
Saint
Nicholas
came with
a bound.

He was dressed
all in fur
from his head
to his foot,
And his clothes
were all tarnished
with ashes and soot.
A bundle of toys
he had flung
on his back,
And he looked
like a peddler
just opening
his pack.

His eyes—how they twinkled!
His dimples—how merry!
His cheeks were like roses,
his nose like a cherry!
His droll little mouth
was drawn up like a bow,
And the beard on his chin
was as white
as the snow.

**The stump of a pipe**
he held tight in his teeth,
And the smoke it encircled
his head like a wreath.
He had a broad face
**and a little round belly**
*That shook when he laughed*
like a bowl full of jelly.
**He was** chubby and plump,
a right jolly old elf,
*And I laughed when I saw him*
*in spite of myself.*

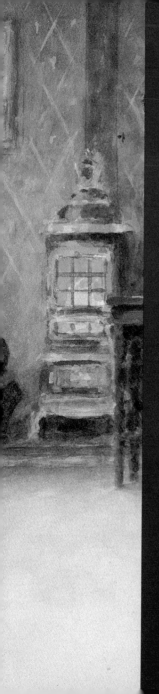

A wink of his eye
and a *twist* of his head
Soon gave me to know
I had nothing to dread.
He spoke not a word
but went straight to his work,
And **filled all
the stockings;**
then turned with a jerk,

And laying his finger
aside of his nose,
*And giving a nod,*
up the chimney
he rose.

He sprang to
his sleigh,
to his team
gave a
whistle,
And away they
all flew
*like the down*
*of a thistle.*
But I heard
him exclaim
ere he drove
out of sight,

"Happy Christmas
to all and to all
a good night!"

Published by Ideals Publications Incorporated
535 Metroplex Drive, Suite 250, Nashville, Tennessee 37211

Printed and bound in Mexico by RR Donnelley & Sons

ISBN 0-8249-4084-9

The display and text type are set in Helvetica Black,
Reckleman, and Berkeley Black.
Color separations by Precision Color Graphics,
New Berlin, Wisconsin

**D e s i g n e d   b y   J o y   C h u**

Second Edition
10 8 6 4   2 3 5 7 9

Library of Congress Cataloging-in-Publication Data

Moore, Clement Clarke, 1779–1863.
     The night before Christmas : the classic poem /
by Clement Clarke Moore ; illustrated by Donald
Mills. — 2nd ed.
       p.  cm.
     Summary: Presents the well-known poem about
an important Christmas visitor.
     ISBN 0-8249-4084-9 (hdbk. : alk. paper).
     1. Santa Claus—Juvenile poetry. 2. Christmas—
Juvenile poetry. 3. Children's poetry, American.
[1. Santa Claus—Poetry. 2. Christmas—Poetry. 3.
American poetry. 4. Narrative poetry.] I. Mills,
Donald, 1896–1974, ill. II. Title.
PS2429.M5N5 1997d
811'.2—dc21                                    97-11482
                                                          CIP
                                                          AC